30 Minutes
...To Write Sales Letters

Ian Linton

KOGAN PAGE

First Indian Edition 2003
Reprinted 2008

Kogan Page India Private Limited
4737/23 Ansari Road,
Daryaganj
New Delhi 110 002

ISBN-10: 81-7554-225-X
ISBN-13: 978-81-7554-225-9

Published by Vinod Vasishtha for Kogan Page India Private Limited, 4737/23 Ansari Road, Daryaganj, New Delhi - 110 002.

Printed and bound at Print Perfect, New Delhi - 110 064.

CONTENTS

The 30 Minutes Series

The Kogan Page 30 Minutes Series has been devised to give your confidence a boost when faced with tackling a new skill or challenge for the first time.

So the next time you're thrown in at the deep end and want to bring your skills up to scratch or pep up your career prospects, turn to the *30 Minutes Series* for help!

Titles available are:
30 Minutes Before A Meeting
30 Minutes Before A Presentation
30 Minutes to Boost Your Communication Skills
30 Minutes to Boost Your Self Esteem
30 Minutes to Brainstorm Great Ideas
30 Minutes to Deal With Difficult People
30 Minutes to Get Your Own Way
30 Minutes to Get Promoted
30 Minutes to Improve Your Networking Skills
30 Minutes to Make the Right Decision
30 Minutes to Manage Your Time Better
30 Minutes to Market Yourself
30 Minutes to Master the Internet
30 Minutes to Motivate Your Staff
30 Minutes to Negotiate a Better Deal
30 Minutes to Plan a Project
30 Minutes to Solve that Problem
30 Minutes to Succeed in Business Writing
30 Minutes to Write a Business Plan
30 Minutes to Write a Marketing Plan
30 Minutes to Write a Report
30 Minutes to Write Sales Letters

Available from all good bookseller.
For further information on the series, please contact:

Kogan Page India Private Limited
2/13, Ansari Road, Daryaganj, New Delhi-110 002
Tel. 23258325, 23279280, 23283121, 23285874, Fax 0091 11 23267224

INTRODUCTION

Managing a sales force can be extremely time-consuming – putting plans together, managing campaigns, letting sales staff and distributors know about new products and campaigns, keeping in touch with key customers.

However, many of these tasks can be handled quickly and efficiently by using a 'system' approach. *30 Minutes to Write Sales Letters* provides a series of time-saving letter templates to help you plan, implement and manage a wide range of sales communication tasks. The approach is flexible enough to be adapted to companies with different levels of sales and marketing expertise and helps you make the most effective use of time and resources.

The scope of a sales letter is much wider than the simple letter selling products or services 'off the page'. The book covers a wide range of letters that help to improve performance at each stage of the sales cycle:

- Selling products and services
- Promoting sales
- Following up a sale

- Maintaining customer contact
- Providing customer information
- Providing product information
- Delivering customer support
- Operating service communications
- Ensuring customer retention
- Improving sales force communications.

You can use this book to improve specific aspects of sales force communications or as the basis for operating a complete sales and customer communications programme.

1

SELLING PRODUCTS AND SERVICES

Send for further information

The most basic type of sales letter offers prospects information on a product or service. In this example, the prospect is offered telecommunications equipment. The prospect is unlikely to buy 'off the page', so the next stage is to contact the company for further information. The letter includes:

- Reassurance about product quality
- Incentive to request further information
- Incentive linked to purchase
- Free response mechanism.

High standards, total reliability, wide choice, nationwide support and the right price. All the qualities you look for when you are purchasing telecommunications equipment.

And all the qualities you'll find in Ringer, the market leading brand in telephone systems and equipment supplied by ABC Communications. With Ringer, you have the widest choice of quality products and systems and you'll find full details in our comprehensive Product Portfolio.

You can be sure that the equipment you buy is right for your business because ABC is the UK's leading supplier of business communications solutions. The Ringer brand has an outstanding reputation for quality and reliability, backed by ABC's nationwide service network providing cover round the clock.

To get the full story on the Ringer brand, send for your complimentary copy of the Ringer Product Portfolio now and receive a voucher worth £500 off your next Ringer order. To take advantage of this offer, fax back or post the attached form, free today.

Selling 'off the page'

Not all sales letters need to move the prospect to the next stage. Simple products can be sold directly 'off the page'. Publishers make extensive use of direct mail to sell magazines or books. In this example, a publisher is offering a directory at substantial savings. The letter includes:

- Benefits of the directory
- Incentive to purchase
- Ordering mechanism.

Targeting new business prospects is key to your continuing success. The *Construction Yearbook* provides a superb basis for building business by helping you to:

- Reach 10,000 named contacts in 3,000 construction companies

- Identify significant purchasing trends in the construction industry
- Review the major product offerings in 250 key industry sectors
- Plan your next marketing campaign.

Now in its 25th edition, the *Construction Yearbook* has been thoroughly researched and updated, saving you time, effort and money on market research.

To save you even more money, the *Construction Yearbook* is available at a special 25 per cent discount if you order before 30 November. Naturally, it comes with a full money back guarantee. If you are not entirely satisfied, simply return the *Yearbook* within 14 days.

To receive your copy, please complete the order form and send it with your payment to the Freepost address above.

PS: The first 25 orders qualify for two free tickets to the Construction Industry Annual Awards Ceremony to be held on 15 January.

Response to an enquiry

When a prospect requests further information, it is an ideal opportunity to reinforce the benefits of the product or service. This extract from a longer letter provides information on a consultancy training programme to prospects who have responded to a press advertisement. The letter describes detailed benefits and encourages the prospect to take action by booking a place. The letter includes:

- Acknowledgement of the enquiry
- Recognition of the prospect's concerns

- Detailed benefits of the service
- Reinforcement of the value of the service
- A simple response mechanism.

Thank you for your enquiry about the Independent Business Programme. We have had the opportunity to talk to many senior executives who, like you, are considering a new career as an independent consultant. Naturally, people in your position have concerns about the change and many have told us they would welcome the opportunity to discuss those concerns with someone who has 'been there and done it'.

We would therefore like to invite you to join one of a series of small group sessions about what it really means to be an independent consultant. The session is free and there is no obligation attached. Each session will consist of about ten people and will be led by a successful independent consultant who has previously held senior positions at board level. It will be carefully structured to give you a comprehensive view of the real world of the independent consultant.

Suddenly you're expected to be a business manager, sales representative, market researcher, accountant and writer – all in the space of a working day. We'll explain how you can cope and where you can get professional support. You will be able to assess for yourself the real benefits of networking. We will also help you to assess your key strengths and weaknesses in relation to your new role. You will be able to discuss any individual concerns with other people in the same situation and with a practising independent consultant. After the session you will have a clearer understanding of the opportunities open to you and the skills you need to focus on for success.

That is what makes the initial session so important. It's vital that you understand your personal strengths and weaknesses and focus on the new skills you need. There is no charge for the session, but we believe this is a valuable investment of your time for the future success of your business. You will have a clear vision of your future and an understanding of what it really means to be an independent consultant.

If you would like to arrange an appointment, please call ... on freephone ...

Targeting individual prospects

Ideally, a sales letter should be written to the recipient as an individual. One-to-one mailing is the logical answer, but this may not always be a practical or cost-effective solution. The letter should reflect, as far as possible, the specific concerns of different decision-makers. In this series of letters, a company is promoting the benefits of videoconferencing to three groups of people who will influence the final purchase decision:

- Managing directors
- Finance directors
- Human resource managers.

Each letter reflects different areas of interest and includes:

- Related experience in the supplier's own company
- Clear business benefits
- Offer of further information or invitation to an event.

Managing director version

I'm sure that, like most managing directors, you want to make the best use of your people and improve your overall business performance.

Our company uses videoconferencing to tackle a range of 'people' issues. We have found that we can develop effective team working, regardless of location, by making full use of videoconferencing. Despite holding more meetings, we have reduced our travel costs significantly, and our clients find the same. As you can see in the reprint of the European article, one of our clients managed to cut their £300,000 annual travel budget in half by using videoconferencing.

We have also noticed wider, more strategic benefits. Videoconferencing meetings are more productive because people stick to business. We find that decision making is quicker and we have been able to reduce our lead times on a number of new product development projects.

I hope that you find this valuable and if you or your colleagues would like to find out more, you are very welcome to attend the launch of our videoconferencing products. You will find details in the accompanying brochure.

Finance director version

Like most finance directors, I am sure you are concerned about the ever-increasing cost of business travel. It seems that the only way to reduce costs is to travel even more to obtain better discounts.

In this company, we face the same problem. With plants around the UK and group offices in Europe, we knew the importance of getting people together to run the business efficiently, but we were also concerned about the level of costs.

Recently, we decided to use some of our own technology to tackle the problem. We now have videoconferencing links throughout the group and I am delighted to say that we have been able to cut our annual business travel budget by around * per cent.

As you can see in the reprint of the European article, one of our clients, a label manufacturer with four plants in different European countries, managed to cut their £300,000 annual travel budget in half by using videoconferencing. The savings are quite significant.

If your company is interested in achieving this level of savings, you or one of your colleagues may like to attend the launch of our videoconferencing products. You will find details in the accompanying brochure.

Human resources manager version

I'm sure that like most human resources professionals, you want to make the best use of your people.

Changes in working practice and new technologies such as videoconferencing mean that we can now adopt a much more flexible approach to location, yet still retain essential contact between people. In this company, we are using videoconferencing to tackle a range of 'people issues' – where should we locate staff, how can we ensure that the right people work together easily and effectively, how can we make the best use of people's time and how can we reduce the inevitable wear and tear of travelling between locations?

Videoconferencing helps bring people together quickly and easily, wherever they are located. We find it extremely valuable too now that an increasing number of people work from home.

I hope that you find this information valuable and if you or your colleagues would like to find out more, you are very welcome to attend the launch of our videoconferencing products. You will find details in the accompanying brochure.

Self-assessment

1. What would you offer to encourage prospects to ask for further information?
2. Which of your company's products would be suitable for selling 'off the page'?
3. What information would you include in a response to a sales enquiry?
4. Who are the main decision-makers for your company's products or services? Which buying factors are most important to each group?

2

FOLLOWING UP A SALE

Welcome letter

The period immediately after a sale provides an ideal opportunity to strengthen customer relationships. A welcome letter allows you to thank the customer for buying the product or service and initiates the next stage in the relationship. This letter accompanies a 'Welcome Pack' which includes guidelines on contacting the company, information on other products and services, special offers and a questionnaire. The letter includes:

- Information on contacting the company
- A summary of the Welcome Pack
- A promise of regular contact
- A reminder to return the questionnaire.

> We are delighted that you have decided to use the Firstrate service. We pride ourselves on offering a

personal service to all our customers and if you would like to discuss any aspect of Firstrate, please contact me or any member of the Customer Service team directly. To help us respond quickly, it would be helpful if you could quote your customer number ... whenever you call.

To help you get the best from your Firstrate system, you will find in your Welcome Pack information on other Firstrate products and services. If you would like more detail on any of these, just give the Customer Service team a call.

I'll be in touch with you regularly to ensure that you are satisfied with the service you are getting from Firstrate and I'll make sure that you are kept up to date with the latest developments in the company. I'll also arrange to meet you once a quarter to review business.

Finally, I would be grateful if you could spend a few minutes completing the questionnaire in the Welcome Pack. It helps us to monitor our performance against your standards and allows us to deal with any concerns you might have. Thank you again for using the Firstrate service. We look forward to working with you to help you take your business forward.

Follow-up offer

Product sales offer an opportunity to build incremental business by offering customers accessories or other items to complement their original purchase. In this example, a power tool customer is offered a discounted subscription to a home improvement magazine. The letter offers a number of important benefits:

- Reinforces the value of the purchase by helping the buyer make better or greater use of the product

- Provides a source of incremental income
- Offers a channel for regular communication with the customer.

You recently bought a hammer drill from our Reading branch and we hope you've been able to put it to good use.

To help you make the most of your drill and tackle some of these really tough jobs, we're offering you a special subscription rate on our new quarterly home improvement magazine, *A Bit on the Side*. Take the first issue with our compliments and enjoy a 10 per cent discount for the rest of the year. And, if you choose to pay your subscriptions by direct debit, you'll receive a free set of masonry bits.

Every issue of the magazine is packed full of great ideas for home improvement and you'll save even more money with our great reader offers. You made a sound investment when you bought that hammer drill and now you can use it to improve your biggest single investment – your home.

Don't delay, the free bit offer lasts until the end of the month, so return the coupon today. Just complete the details and post it – you won't need a stamp.

PS: If you need any more accessories for your drill, there's a sale on at your local branch.

Offering the customer an extended warranty

The offer of an extended warranty demonstrates customer care and increases customer retention after the sale. Although customers are normally given a guarantee when they purchase the product, the point of purchase is an ideal time to sell an extended warranty. If the customer does not take up the offer immediately, you should continue offering the facility whenever you are in contact with the customer; for example, when the guarantee expires or the product is due for service. This letter reinforces the benefits of the extended warranty and informs the customer of the timescale for signing up.

It's not too late to enjoy peace of mind with Cover Care.

If you didn't take out Cover Care when you bought your new washing machine, there's still time. Your first year guarantee expires on ..., but you can continue to enjoy many of the benefits by taking out Cover Care within the next 30 days.

Cover Care provides you with complete peace of mind against unexpected repair costs and gives you the additional benefit of priority call out for the period of cover. There is a choice of three Cover Care plans to suit your needs and we'll be delighted to discuss which one is most suitable.

You'll find full details of Cover Care in the leaflet enclosed. If you would like to enjoy the reassurance of complete peace of mind, contact ... now.

Assessing satisfaction with the sales process

Many customer satisfaction questionnaires concentrate on the customer's views of the product. However, the period after the sale provides an opportunity to assess how well the sales process is working. This questionnaire asks for the customer's views on the sales process within a retail outlet.

Thank you for sparing a few minutes to fill in our

customer service questionnaire. Your responses are of great value to us in identifying areas where we can improve our service to you. When you have completed the form please return it in the stamped addressed envelope provided.

1. While you were in the showroom, did a member of staff acknowledge you? YES/NO
2. Did the sales person introduce him/herself? YES/NO
3. Which of the following questions did the salesperson ask?
   - Style/range required YES/NO
   - Budget YES/NO
   - Accessories required YES/NO
4. Did the salesperson provide any of the following?
   - Brochure YES/NO
   - Details of the guarantee YES/NO
   - Price YES/NO
   - Business card YES/NO
5. How satisfied were you with the sales/service you received? Very satisfied
Fairly satisfied
Not satisfied

If you would like to make any further comments please use the space below.

Self-assessment

1. What type of information would you include in a customer welcome pack?
2. What would you offer customers as a follow-up to the sale?

3. What benefits would an extended warranty offer your customers?
4. Which elements of the sales process could you assess via a customer questionnaire?

3

MAINTAINING CUSTOMER CONTACT

After the sale is over and you have welcomed the customer, how do you maintain contact until the next sale? This and subsequent chapters describe a number of ways to increase the level of communication with your customers. In this chapter, we look at the concept of a 'customer club'. Regular customers receive information and special offers, ideally targeted to their individual purchasing patterns. As well as maintaining contact, a club also provides an opportunity to build up an increasingly detailed picture of the customer.

The 'Colour Club' described in this chapter is aimed at companies offering vehicle accident repair services and is operated by a company manufacturing refinishing paint systems. A series of letters is used to encourage participation in the club, make special offers and provide update information.

Introductory letter

This letter is sent to existing customers, inviting them to join the Colour Club. It describes the benefits of the club and includes an incentive to join.

You are a valued long-term customer, so we'd like to invite your company to become a member of our new Colour Club.

As one of the privileges of membership, your bodyshop will receive the most comprehensive, up-to-date colour support on the market, using sophisticated techniques to put the latest information in your hands as soon as it's available. What's more, you'll be able to take advantage of pre-launch access to the latest special basecoat tinters, plus an exciting new concept in colour information – the *Colour Yearbook*, offered free to members.

And, there's much, much more than colour benefits. Through the Colour Club, your business will ...

Save, with discounts off a range of bodyshop services:

— bodyshop design services, using the latest in computer-aided design to improve layout and workflow

— computerised bodyshop estimating and reporting systems, ensuring your profits are right.

Profit, from advanced colour retrieval systems:

— discounts on computerised colour retrieval systems to replace microfiche

— discounts on Car-Mix scales to help manage the materials in your mixing room.

Develop, through special deals on training courses for your staff:

— including a free introductory voucher for one course, valued at £175.

Grow through sharing knowledge with other bodyshop professionals and relax at Club meetings combining business and pleasure.

All this adds up to an opportunity that's too good to miss. For a simple subscription of just £99 per year, your business can profit from this superb range of offers. And, if you join before 12 November, you can get your membership off to a flying start. Your company's name will be entered in a prize draw. And, as the official representative of your company, you could be the lucky winner of a trip for two couples to the Bodytalk exhibition in Dallas, Texas in December.

So don't delay, we look forward to welcoming you and your company into the Colour Club. Just complete the enclosed application form and return it to us now. And don't forget, if you join before 12 November, you could qualify for that special prize.

Welcome letter

This letter is issued to new members. It reinforces the benefits of the programme and provides essential membership information.

Welcome to the Colour Club. We're delighted that you have decided to join the growing number of companies who are taking advantage of our advanced colour information and special offers to improve their colour confidence in the bodyshop.

You'll find enclosed everything you need to get started, plus details of some special offers that we hope will help you improve bodyshop performance even further. Don't forget to tell your customers about your membership. Membership shows that you are committed to the highest standards of colour accuracy, which we believe will help to build customer confidence and satisfaction.

Look out for further offers and regular updates on colour information because the privileges of membership have only just begun. This is just the first stage in an ongoing partnership. We'll carry on talking to you to find out about your changing needs and we'll continue to develop the Colour Club so it provides you with the colour confidence you want.

We hope to see you at one of the Colour Club social events and if you have any queries or comments, please let us know.

Event information

This letter accompanies a programme of club events for the forthcoming year. By including events, the company increases opportunities to meet customers face to face.

When we first discussed the concept of the Colour Club, you told us loud and clear that the Club should be for people. You wanted the opportunity to meet fellow professionals in relaxed surroundings, with the emphasis on mixing business with pleasure.

Next year's seminar programme will bring people in the business together to listen, learn and ask about key issues like ISO 9001, the Environmental Protection Act and investment in training. We were delighted at the response to last year's programme, and we will continue to make seminars a key part of our future strategy.

Customer update

This letter keeps customers up to date with company and product developments. Members are given advance information on new products, as well as privileged access to special services as they are introduced.

You told us that you wanted to be kept up to date on colour issues. Technical information is an integral element of the Club service, and we'll keep you abreast of the latest product and environmental developments as well as new colour information available before the next edition of the *Yearbook*.

To make sure you've got the information at your fingertips as quickly as possible, we'll be using the 'Fast Fax' service. And don't forget, as a member you'll have privileged access to our Freephone Colour Club Hotline for immediate advice from colour specialists.

You wanted up-to-date information on new bodyshop systems to help you stay ahead of the competition. As well as value-for-money colour information, we will be providing you with pre-launch access to the latest basecoat tinters which provide the 'exotic' colours increasingly used in today's range of car colours. These tinters are not generally available on the market, but we are offering them exclusively to Colour Club members.

Members' competition

This competition offers members a prize that will benefit their business – a trip to a trade exhibition in the USA. The letter explains the scope of the prize and includes entry details.

Win a trip to Dallas in December.

We're taking two couples to Bodytalk – the international vehicle repair exhibition. Like everything else in Texas, it's reckoned to be the biggest and best. This is THE international refinishing event – the world's biggest bodyshop show with over 2000 booths – and you'll have time to take it all in and enjoy the best of Texan hospitality.

The lucky winners will fly direct to Dallas on 1 December and stay till 7 December in a superb hotel. Thursday will be a free day to give you and your partner a taste of Texas and later on you'll have a chance to meet other visitors at a special Welcome Party.

Friday, Saturday and Sunday are show days and we've organised a programme of events to help you make the most of the vast selection of exhibits, seminars and workshops. The show closes at 2.00 Sunday so you'll have the afternoon free and, on Monday, we've arranged an optional tour of local bodyshops to give you a first-hand view of American practice. While you're taking all this in, we'll also be taking care of your partners, with visits and tours designed to help you make the most of this exciting glamorous city.

All good things come to an end, unfortunately, and you'll fly back on 7 December, raring to put your new ideas into practice in your bodyshop. We're sure Bodytalk will be an experience to remember and it's a great way to say welcome to the Colour Club.

So don't delay: make sure you return your entry form before 12 November. We'll be drawing the names of the lucky winners on 17 November.

Offer of training vouchers

The overall aim of the Colour Club is to offer members services that benefit their business. In this letter, members are offered vouchers entitling them to discounts on training programmes. The letter describes the business benefits of training and outlines the facilities available.

Successful companies recognise that improved business performance cannot be achieved by good management alone. It's essential to energise every employee to make the most of their talents – and training is the vital ingredient.

To help you take advantage of the superb training facilities available, we have enclosed a voucher which entitles you to one day's free colour skills training for a member of your staff at our Skills Centre.

The Skills Centre is committed to leadership in training for the refinishing industry. The Centre develops courses that meet the real needs of professional bodyshops in the 1990s and delivers training in a way that is efficient, convenient and cost-effective. Our aim is to help your staff get the best possible results from our paint system. The benefit to you is a consistently high standard of performance and satisfied bodyshop customers.

Because the refinishing business is highly technical, we balance our practical hands-on training approach with sound theory. We aim to give every delegate an understanding of the potential of paint systems and ensure they are familiar with new bodyshop technology, as well as the environmental and safety implications of modern refinishing systems.

If you would like more details of training courses available at the Skills Centre, please call the Colour

Club helpline. To book your complimentary place on the colour skills course, call the Skills Centre direct, quoting your Colour Club membership number.

Self-assessment

1. What form would a customer club for your organisation take?
2. What services and special offers would be appropriate to your members?
3. How could you use events to increase contact with customers?
4. How you encourage customers to take advantage of your training services?

4

CUSTOMER INFORMATION

Customers need to be confident that your company can continue to provide them with a quality reliable service, so they need to be kept up to date with developments in the company. Information on new appointments, new services, investment plans, financial performance and future direction are vital elements of the customer communication process.

New appointment letter

This letter introduces a new representative. It provides personal background and also outlines other business developments that will help to improve customer service. The letter is designed to build the client's confidence.

I'd like to introduce myself as your new Parts Specialist. I'll be taking personal responsibility for your parts business and I'd appreciate the opportunity to meet you soon to discuss how we can further improve our service to you. Although I have just started this new position, I'm no stranger to the business. I've worked here for three years and it's a great opportunity to be able to work closely with our parts customers.

As you probably know, we recently completed the refurbishment of our parts office – more telephone lines, more people and more stock. We can now deal with your enquiries and orders promptly and efficiently. We've increased our loading area so that we can get our delivery vans on the road quickly to meet those urgent requests. We've also put all of our parts staff through a customer service training programme, so we hope you're already noticing the difference.

If you have any concerns, or if there are aspects of our parts service that you would like to discuss, now is the time to do it. I'll be taking personal responsibility for your business, so I'll make sure we make the changes and stick to them.

I look forward to meeting you soon and will contact you shortly to arrange a meeting.

New sales support arrangements

As well as new sales appointments, you should also keep your customers informed about the levels of support they can obtain from the sales force. In this letter, an office automation company introduces a range of consultancy services available to the customer. This enhances the credibility of the team and increases the opportunity for customer contact.

We understand the growing complexities you face in choosing and using office automation products, so we have set up a team of specialist sales consultants to provide you with professional sales, service and administrative support.

They can help you understand how changing organisational patterns, emerging technologies, the growth of multi-functional systems and new working methods affect office systems and ensure that our solutions are flexible enough to meet your changing requirements throughout a contract period.

The team will hold regular review meetings with you to identify future requirements and to assess the performance and capacity of installed systems. If you are relocating or requirements alter, they can develop a cost-effective plan for managing the change. The growth of digital technology and the increasing convergence of different technologies provide new opportunities for increased quality, productivity and efficiency. The team will brief you on new developments and help you to identify opportunities for exploiting technology.

Your personal sales consultant will be contacting you shortly to arrange a preliminary meeting.

Letter about new retail outlet

If you are opening a new retail outlet, let customers know about the location, opening hours and facilities available. This letter explains the improvements in customer service that the new outlet will bring and also informs customers about any interim arrangements while building work is taking place.

The complete refurbishment of our Sheffield dealership is progressing on target and is scheduled for completion in June of this year. When the work is completed, the complex will provide facilities for new and used vehicle sales, service, parts and accident repair on one convenient site.

This is the culmination of a three-year, £2 million investment that will enable us to deliver the highest standards of service, whatever our customers want. Response to the new showrooms at York Road has been very positive and our service and repair customers will soon be able to enjoy the same standards.

When it is completed, the York Road complex will offer a number of brand new services – a car wash, a retail shop offering a wide range of parts and accessories, MoT testing and a convenient drive-in service for exhausts, tyres and batteries for all makes of car.

Widening the range of services available to customers is an important part of the new development. We can now service and repair vehicles of any make to manufacturers' standards. Business customers who operate mixed fleets appreciate the convenience and flexibility of having all the work done at one site and we can offer the same facilities to private owners.

While the building work progresses, it is business as usual. The complex is taking shape already. The site has been cleared and the footings are now in place. With the prospects of better building weather coming up, the appearance of York Road could change dramatically over the next few months. We will keep you in touch with developments.

Letter explaining contact procedures

Are you certain that your customers can reach the right contact when they call? By simplifying the contact procedure, you can enhance the quality of customer service.

This letter explains how contact has been simplified through the use of Freephone numbers and a single point of contact.

Enclosed is your personal Calling Card. You can use it to contact us with any queries or service requests. Whenever you want to contact us, all you have to do is dial the special 0800 number on the card.

You'll get straight through to a member of the Customer Service team and there will be no charge for the call. Don't forget to quote your customer number when you call.

The Customer Service team will deal initially with all your enquiries, including:

- Technical queries
- Service requests
- Order processing
- Invoice queries
- General queries
- Product information.

A member of the Customer Service team will take the call and establish your exact requirements. If the Customer Service representative cannot deal with the enquiry, you will be transferred to an appropriate specialist.

Your customer number plus the free 0800 number provides you with a convenient, single point of contact for all services. We hope you will find it easy to use.

Letter about new ways to obtain information

You can use technology to enhance the way you deliver service and provide information to your customers. Here, an engineering company is using a fax distribution service to speed up the process of issuing technical updates.

You can't get information much quicker than this unless you join the information superhighway. If you've got a fax machine, you'll receive up-to-date technical information on our products as soon as it's available. Before Fastfax, the only way to get detailed information out quickly was to get on the telephone or send our sales representatives out with printed material when it was available. Fastfax eliminates any delay.

Last year we faxed advice on technical changes and service information that proved valuable to many of our customers. One engineering manager told us, 'We had to modify a service procedure and we couldn't find any reference. The latest Fastfax came that morning and it had just the information we needed'.

Don't forget to put the Fastfax in your Fastfax File as soon as it arrives – you never know when you might need it.

Letter about a company's future plans

Telling your customers about your plans for the future helps build their confidence and lays the foundation for long-term relationship. By outlining your plans for investment and improvement, your customers are assured that you can continue to provide them with a quality service. In this letter, a computer services company introduces a brochure which outlines their 'vision' for the future.

Our vision: Every client recommends Complus.

People might say that's a tall order, but that's our goal. So, if you're looking for a partner to help you set the pace and maintain leadership in your market, it's time we talked.

When we ask customers how they see our role, they tell us 'we do for businesses all the things they are too smart to do for themselves'. Because we handle the processing and all the back office functions that can tie up your valuable resources, your staff are free to concentrate on driving your business forward.

We realise we're taking on a great responsibility in handling this business for you, so we'd like to tell you more about our commitment to quality customer service and our strategic direction. Continuous improvement is at the heart of everything we do and, in setting the pace, every action is driven by a desire to achieve the highest levels of customer satisfaction.

In this brochure, you will find a brief outline of the services we offer. It's only a starting point because we want to get to know your business. When we start talking, you'll see what we mean by partnership. Before long, we hope that you'll be one of the clients who recommend Complus.

Self-assessment

1. Do you keep customers up to date with new appointments?
2. Have you introduced new sales arrangements which will improve customer service?
3. Are you opening new retail outlets? What impact will they have on customer service?
4. Do your customers find it easy to contact your organisation?
5. Are your customers aware of your organisation's future plans?

5

PRODUCT INFORMATION

Assessing customers' information needs

Are you certain that your customers have all the information they need on your products and services? A car dealership talked to local customers informally and discovered that few customers were aware of the full extent of the services available from the dealership. This letter acted partly as a market research tool and partly as a means of raising awareness and generating additional business for the dealership.

What do Anytown Motors do? Tell us and take part in our Christmas draw.

A lot of people think we just sell and repair cars. In fact, we do resprays, hire cars, sell tyres and exhausts, sell petrol, carry out MoT tests and a whole lot more.

Most people don't realise that, so we'd like to hear what you think about Anytown Motors. If you'd like to complete this questionnaire, pop it in the post or drop it into the forecourt shop, we'll enter your name into a free draw for a Christmas hamper. You don't have to buy anything; all we want is your opinion.

What do Anytown Motors do?
Please return to Anytown Motors
Name ... Address ... Telephone ...
Make and model of car ... Registration ...

Our services
(Please tick the services you think we offer)

Scheduled service	☐	Repairs	☐
Exhaust fitting	☐	Tyre fitting	☐
MoT tests	☐	Car hire	☐
Used car sales	☐	New car sales	☐
Resprays	☐	Safety checks	☐
Courtesy cars	☐	Accident repairs	☐
Breakdown recovery	☐	Oil and filter change	☐
Petrol	☐	Accessories	☐

New product announcement letter

When you announce a product that incorporates new technology or a new approach to existing problems, you may have to educate customers. This letter is promoting a database service used to solve crime and fraud in the financial services sector. The letter focuses on simplicity of use, as well as the effectiveness of the product.

How quickly and easily can you investigate raids and fraud cases?

Whether you're a financial institution suffering from fraud or raids, or a police force investigating an incident, it would be easier to 'get a result' if you could quickly obtain data from different incidents for comparison. If you've got a personal computer, you could have the data you need on your desktop within minutes. High quality stills and video images, together with comprehensive information on dates, times, locations and suspect details are there on your screen. Establishing links between separate events becomes easier and patterns quickly become evident, helping you not only to solve cases quickly, but also to plan preventative measures.

The vital support you need is Crimesolver, a unique security database that is constantly updated and provides access to records of thousands of raids or fraud cases. Data that has been fully cross-referenced can be transmitted anywhere in the country over high-quality digital telephone lines and is available for use immediately.

Specially developed software running on your personal computer allows you to enter details of specific incidents and search the database for information on repeat incidents or offenders. The high quality images and comprehensive data available on your screen speed up investigation and reduce wasted effort. The software offers high levels of security, as well as powerful search facilities.

For more information or a demonstration of Crimesolver, please contact ...

Letter about range extension

A new product announcement provides an opportunity to remind customers about the rest of the range and to demonstrate your organisation's commitment to continuous improvement. This letter from an oil company accompanies a magazine which describes the full product range as well as the new products.

We are delighted that you have been using products from the Flow range. Since their launch in 1993, Flow oils have become a firm favourite with customers around the country and this year oil sales are forecast to exceed 1 million litres.

Feedback from our customers indicates that price, service and quality are the main reasons for choosing Flow oils. We are therefore pleased to announce that the Flow range is being extended even further in line with your needs.

In this issue of *Flow News*, you will find details of the full Flow range – a single source of quality branded products for the aftermarket including engine, gear and transmission oils, plus workshop consumables such as brake and carburettor cleaners, absorbent granules, hand cleansers and safety gloves.

You will also find information about new products currently in the pipeline plus information on marketing and technical support programmes. If you haven't tried the full range of Flow products, you can order a special launch pack which covers the full range and comes with a bonus of 50 300 ml packs of Screen Wash free of charge. For the full story on Flow products, contact your area manager now.

Upgrading an existing product

A customer who has invested in a high value product may not want to replace it in the short term. However, by offering the customer upgrades, you can provide product enhancement and increase revenue between major sales. In this letter, a telephone manufacturer explains the benefits and the practicalities of upgrading.

You made a shrewd decision when you bought

System 1. You invested in a system which can grow with your business.

With over 5 million lines installed in 40 countries, System 1 has built a reputation for quality, reliability and superb engineering, providing users with the connectivity and flexibility to support voice, data, text and video over existing telephone lines.

Since its introduction, System 1 has been continually enhanced through software upgrades to provide ever greater functionality. Developments such as Voice Mail, ISDN, Automatic Call Distribution, Computer-Telephony Integration and Cordless Telephony increase efficiency and improve the quality of customer service.

Upgrading is a simple, cost-effective process that will allow you to protect your investment in System 1 and take full advantage of the latest developments in telecommunications without changing your existing infrastructure. Users do not have to retrain: they can use the same documentation, and the user interface is unchanged.

The accompanying booklet explains how you can upgrade your existing system and describes the cost, service, flexibility and productivity benefits of both new and existing System 1 features.

If you would like to find out how easy it is to upgrade System 1, contact your account manager.

Self-assessment

1. Are customers aware of all the products and services you offer?
2. How important is customer education to your new product launch programme?
3. Can you use upgrades to increase sales to existing customers?

6

CUSTOMER SUPPORT

Providing your customers with advice, information and support can help to improve relationships.

Dealing with customer queries

Customers don't always know where to get information and advice. This letter from a financial services company explains the support service available and how to use it.

> We understand that from time to time you have queries about your financial arrangements and you would like to talk to someone straight away.
>
> You might want to know whether your present level of cover is sufficient to allow for a change in circumstances. Perhaps you are not clear about some aspect of your personal plan. You may want advice on further investment or other forms of savings. You're filling in your tax return and you need advice. If your budget gets tight, you may want advice on postponing premiums or surrendering a policy. You

may just want information on other products and services.

Whatever the query, support and helpful personal advice is just a phone call away. Call the Customer Service Helpdesk on 0800 123456 any time of the day or night and you'll get an immediate response. Up to 8.00 pm on weekdays or 1.00 pm on Saturday, we'll deal with your query straight away. If it's later, we'll call you back next working day.

We have products and services to meet a wide range of needs, including:

- Protection
- Savings
- Pensions
- Mortgage policies
- Investments.

If you want information on any of these, contact the Helpdesk on 0800 123456.

Offering customers a management guide

To help them run their businesses effectively, companies need concise, up-to-date information on new developments in their industry. In this letter, a distribution company is offering customers a guide to the latest logistics techniques. The offer demonstrates the company's expertise in distribution and helps to strengthen customer relationships.

Recent research has shown that effective distribution is a key factor in ensuring profitability in the food industry. If you want to improve your distribution management, you'll find the enclosed report,

Distribution – The Way Ahead, a valuable guide to planning the development of your own systems.

It deals with the key issues facing distribution managers and includes case histories showing how six leading companies have used our logistics software to turn distribution into a competitive weapon.

To help you take the next step towards successful distribution management, we're offering a free consultation with a leading independent expert to every customer who orders a system.

To take advantage of this special offer, please contact your account manager on Freephone …

Invitation to a seminar

Seminars, like management guides, demonstrate a company's expertise and provide an excellent opportunity for high level contact with different members of a customer's decision-making team. In this letter, a training consultancy is promoting a series of management development seminars.

'Driving for growth': Is your management team stuck in the slow lane?

Many companies talk about growth, but few are really achieving it. They blame the government, economic conditions, the City, the consumer … But how many companies really bother to look on their own doorstep: at their own management team?

Is your management team developing your business or protecting their jobs? A cautious management team is hardly a recipe for innovation, creativity and growth. How do you overcome the inertia? We believe that in every organisation, there is a small group of dynamic ambitious managers with the positive attitude you need to move forward.

Dynamic managers stand out easily. They're ambitious, they innovate, they motivate their people, they frequently irritate their colleagues. You recognise them by their attitude. Managers with attitude don't always have the 'right qualifications'. They might be MBAs or they might have no formal qualifications, but they've got 'the right stuff'.

In the next few days, we'll be contacting you to explain how a series of development seminars, 'Driving for growth', can harness their talents and enhance their skills so that they can act as dynamic catalysts for change in your organisation.

In the meantime, check that these people have got free dates in their diary next March.

Helping customers deal with legislation

Many industries face increasingly stringent legislation which can put up costs and change working practices. By offering customers advice and practical support, a supplier can demonstrate responsibility and high levels of customer care. In this letter, a paint manufacturer acknowledges the problems customers face in dealing with environmental legislation. The letter not only helps to improve customer relations, it also provides an opportunity to gain valuable market information.

Will your business survive the new, tougher, environmental laws?

We can't answer that question for you, but we can go a long way towards helping you. Because we're so closely involved with the refinishing business, we understand the increasing pressure you face from environmental legislation. We know that reducing solvent emission levels won't just change the materials you use, it could cost you your business. Fortunately, we recognised the risks before the new guidelines became law and we have developed a solution that protects both the environment *and* the interests of the refinishing trade. The solution will enable you to comply with emission levels today without investing or changing the way you paint.

It costs nothing to find out more, so here are three steps you can take towards a more secure future:

- ☐ Please send me an information pack
- ☐ Call me to arrange a discussion with an environment specialist
- ☐ Book a place for me at the nearest seminar in June/July

It would help us review your individual needs more efficiently if you could take a moment to complete a few simple questions:

1. Are you currently negotiating with your local environmental officer?
2. Are you considering a move to new refinishing technology?
3. What is your current level of emissions?
4. Are you able to meet new emission levels?

Helping customers to make better decisions

When companies are purchasing new technology, they are often uncertain how it will affect their business or their working practices. Advice and guidance before the purchase can reduce risk and uncertainty. In this letter, a document management company offers prospects a checklist that can be used to evaluate the benefits of new technology.

This checklist is designed to help you assess the contribution document image processing could make to your organisation. Ideally, you should set up a team including senior managers, user departments and IT specialists to review your requirements.

We can support your review by carrying out a free assessment of your requirements together with free processing of your sample documents. If you would like to take advantage of this offer, please return the completed form.

1. Electronic image processing is ideal for improving the efficiency and productivity of high volume activities. Which of these is most important to your organisation?

   Correspondence — Purchasing

   Accounts — Personnel

   Technical engineering libraries — Other

2. To calculate the potential cost/benefits, it is worth focusing on critical activities:

   Which activity do you feel would benefit most from document management?

   How many users would be involved?

   What is the approximate volume of documents per week/month?

   What are the current storage requirements for this activity?

3. Electronic image processing can be used to create electronic documents from a variety of source

materials. Which of these items is your main source material?

Letters
Purchase orders
Faxes
Press cuttings
Reports
Microfilm
35 mm slides
Videos
Invoices
Delivery notes
E-mail
Books
Drawings
Digital images
Audio tapes

4. Documents can be easily shared between different users and departments. Which of these working patterns are important to you?

Workflow
Parallel working
Supplier/sub-contractor partnerships
Team working
Simultaneous engineering
Multiple sites

5. Electronic image processing solutions can be integrated with business applications and other information systems. What type of integration is important to you?

Corporate network
Word processing
Project management
Mobile data
Accounts
Database management

6. Electronic imaging solutions can be integrated with existing databases or document management products. Do you need to integrate with any of the following?

Packaged document management software
Stand-alone document processing equipment
Microfilm systems

7. Effective electronic image processing depends on a number of key processes. Do you have any of the following resources within your organisation?

Consultancy and solution design	Application development Customisation
Implementation	Systems integration
Project management	Training
System maintenance	Indexing
Document processing	Data migration from databases
Conversion from microfilm	

To take advantage of the free assessment and sample processing, please post or fax the completed form.

Self-assessment

1. Are your customers aware of support services available to them?
2. What type of management guides would be appropriate to your customers?
3. How could you use seminars to improve customer relationships?
4. Would checklists help your customers make better-informed decisions?

7

CUSTOMER RETENTION

It costs less to retain existing customers than to win new ones. Part of the customer retention process is resolving problems promptly and following up any customer complaints.

Problem follow-up letters

This series of letters covers a range of different scenarios faced by many organisations. The customer has a problem which is either resolved immediately or requires further action.

Version 1: Problem now solved
Thank you for letting us know that you are now fully satisfied with ...

While we aim to achieve the highest standards from the outset, we understand that problems can occur and we are pleased that you took the trouble to bring it to our attention.

We aim to respond positively to our customers' concerns and will be looking very closely at the particular process that was used.

We hope that you will use our services in the future and we look forward to dealing with you. Thank you once again for contacting us.

Version 2: Unable to contact customer

You recently contacted us about …

I wanted to discuss this with you personally over the telephone, but I have been unable to reach you. If you would like to contact … (name/number of contact who can take calls) and let them know when we can reach you, I will call you back.

I am sorry to hear that you have a problem and I would like to settle the matter as quickly as possible. While we aim to achieve the highest standards from the outset, we understand that problems can occur and we are pleased that you took the trouble to bring it to our attention.

We aim to respond positively to our customers' concerns and will be looking very closely at the particular process that was used. Thank you once again for contacting us and I hope to speak to you very soon.

Version 3: Problem doing the rounds

You recently contacted us about … and I understand that you have not yet had a satisfactory reply. I am sorry that there has been a delay and I am now taking personal responsibility for the matter.

EITHER

I wanted to discuss this with you personally over the telephone, but I have been unable to reach you. If you would like to contact ... (name/number of a contact who can take calls) and let them know when we can reach you, I will call you back.

OR

I want to discuss this with you personally over the telephone, and I will be contacting you in the next few days.

I hope that we can then settle the matter as quickly as possible. While we aim to achieve the highest standards from the outset, we understand that problems can occur and we are pleased that you took the trouble to bring it to our attention.

We aim to respond positively to our customers' concerns and will be looking very closely at the particular process that was used. Thank you once again for contacting us and I hope to speak to you very soon.

Version 4: Problem needs specialist reply

You recently contacted us about ... and I understand that you have not yet had a satisfactory reply. I am sorry that there has been a delay and I am now taking personal responsibility for the matter.

Your query is being investigated by a specialist in ... department and I have asked that person to report back to me within ... days. I will then telephone you to discuss the matter and, if necessary, arrange for the specialist to contact you directly.

I hope that we can then settle the matter as quickly as possible. While we aim to achieve the highest standards from the outset, we understand that problems can occur and we are pleased that you took the trouble to bring it to our attention.

We aim to respond positively to our customers'

concerns and we will be looking very closely at the particular process that was used. Thank you once again for contacting us and I hope to speak to you very soon.

Winning back lost customers

Even if customers indicate that they no longer wish to buy from a company, there is still an opportunity to win back the business. Even if the customer decides not to continue, the company has demonstrated that it takes a positive attitude to customer service. These two letters indicate different approaches to regaining business.

Letter 1

I'd like to introduce myself as your new account manager and would appreciate the opportunity to meet you soon to discuss how we can perhaps win back your business by improving our service to you.

First, let me bring you up to date with what has been happening in the company. As you probably know, we recently completed the refurbishment of our sales department – more telephone lines, more people and more stock. We can now deal with your enquiries and orders promptly and efficiently. We've increased our loading area so that we can get our delivery vans on the road quickly to meet those urgent requests. We also put all of our sales staff through a customer service training programme, so we hope you'll notice the difference if you try us again.

What is really important is to look at your individual needs more closely and to find out why you stopped using us. Was it deliveries? The discount structure? Did you find it difficult to get through to us, or were there other problems that need to be resolved?

If you have any concerns or if there are aspects of our service that you would like to discuss, now is the time to do it. I'll be taking personal responsibility for your business, so I'll make sure we make the changes and stick to them.

Our attitude to business is 'service first' so we want to make sure that we get that right first time, every time. It would really help us to achieve this if you could take a little time to fill in the questionnaire that comes with this letter. I can then discuss it with the management team and develop a personal action plan for your business.

We really would like to win your business back, so we hope that you will allow us to make a quote or, better still, try us out for a month. We believe you'll notice the difference straight away.

I will contact you shortly to arrange a meeting.

QUESTIONNAIRE

We would welcome the opportunity to handle your business again and we want to ensure that you enjoy the highest standards of service. So that we can meet your individual requirements, we would be grateful if you could take the time to complete this questionnaire. Please return it to ... at address or fax number ...

Did you find it easy to contact us by phone?

Did you use our fax ordering service?

Did our staff answer your queries efficiently?

Were we able to fulfil your orders on time?

How many daily deliveries do you need?

Would you prefer one source for all your purchases?

Were you satisfied with the accuracy of our invoicing?

Would you like to see improvements in any of the following areas:

— price/discounts

— delivery timing

— delivery frequency

— information on products

— information on special offers

— information about the company

Letter 2

I was very concerned to hear that you no longer wish to buy from us. I'm sorry about the delay in getting back to you, but I have only returned from holiday today.

As you know we have been working together for almost ... years and I felt that we had an extremely good working relationship. We have aimed to provide you with the highest standards of service during that period and I have not been aware of any serious problems.

I was therefore extremely surprised to hear that you have taken your business elsewhere for no apparent reason We are always willing to discuss any factors that might affect the relationship – price, delivery, quality, discounts or anything else – but on this occasion we have not been given the opportunity to do so.

The directors and I value our long working relationship with your company and we would appreciate an opportunity to discuss the situation with you. Hopefully, we will be able to resolve any issues that may be concerning you. I will call you within the next few days to arrange a meeting.

Self-assessment

1. Do you have a policy for customer retention?
2. Do you have procedures for dealing with customer complaints?
3. Do you continue to communicate with lost customers?
4. Do you ask your customers whether you meet their service requirements?

8

SALES FORCE COMMUNICATIONS

Regular communication with the sales force ensures that they understand products, markets, competitors and marketing opportunities.

New product announcement

Sales force commitment is crucial to the success of a product launch. Unless the sales force put enough effort into the launch, they will not reach their launch targets and could lose momentum. But to launch the new product effectively, the sales force must believe in it; they must be convinced that it will benefit their customers.

> Research shows that there is pent-up demand for a technically advanced product. We have designed our new product range to meet and exceed the requirements shown in the research programme and we believe prospects will be extremely receptive to this initiative.

To help you generate interest in the marketplace, we will be running a press information programme with feature articles on the technical performance of the new product range. We will also make available a number of demonstration models which can be offered to important customers for a trial period. We believe that this will generate high levels of interest in the marketplace and make your task more manageable.

The new product range represents a considerable advance in performance over the current range and will enable us to compete as a technically advanced supplier. To help you explain the benefits of the range, we have prepared a detailed product guide which includes full product information, together with background on the market and competitors. The guide has been structured for use as a sales presentation aid, with clear benefit statements and strong graphics to highlight key features of the product. We will also be running a series of product workshops so that you can see the product in action and learn how to demonstrate it.

To reward members of the sales force who exceed their launch targets, we will be operating a structured incentive programme which includes a number of different elements. Points will be awarded for key account demonstrations, sales and after-market sales of service contracts. We will also be awarding points for levels of product knowledge to ensure that you have the skills to present the product effectively.

Explaining a sales programme

With any sales programme, it is essential that the sales team understand the benefits and operation of the programme. In some cases, it may be necessary to provide the equivalent of a brief 'operating guide'.

Customer Connection is an exciting new customer retention programme designed to strengthen and enhance relationships with new and existing customers. The programme, which is effective 1 August, builds on the success of Customer Care, replacing it with a highly-targeted programme of regular, timely and relevant communications.

Through Customer Connection, we will seize the initiative in customer satisfaction, regaining leadership and moving ahead of competitors who were beginning to catch us up. For the first time, the customer retention programme targets owners by product. It also encourages feedback through surveys and helplines, enabling us to build dialogue with our customers. Customer Connection will deliver a number of important benefits:

- Strengthen customer loyalty
- Improve the frequency and quality of customer contact
- Enable us to treat customers as individuals
- Provide more information about customers' specific requirements and attitudes
- Build a more complete picture of prospects for future sales
- Ensure that the communications process operates effectively.

Although the Customer Connection is operated centrally, you need to be aware of the key stages so that you can take full advantage of the programme. Here is a suggested personal action planner:

1. Make sure you have ordered sufficient quantities of the programme material
2. Familiarise yourself with its contents
3. Make sure all the relevant documentation is completed ready for the handover
4. Note the dates of the various mailings
5. Make a courtesy call to customers to ensure they received their material on the appropriate dates
6. Follow up any queries or concerns arising from the customer survey
7. Follow up any mailings.

The Customer Connection gives us a head start in treating our customers and prospects as individuals. The programme is designed to evolve into an even more powerful direct marketing tool that will enable us to communicate with customers on a one-to-one basis in the long term. One-to-one marketing at that level will play a crucial role in retaining customers for life.

Questions and answers

Q. Why has the programme been introduced?

A. To give us greater insight into our customers' needs and to enhance the quality and frequency of customer communications. Customer satisfaction surveys were telling us that competitors were beginning to catch us up in after-care.

Q. Does the programme apply only to new customers? What about existing owners?

A. Some elements of the programme, such as the quarterly magazines, customer survey and in-market material will be mailed to existing owners at the appropriate time.

Q. How do new customers get on to the programme?
A. They are automatically registered when we receive the copy invoice.
Q. What do I have to do?
A. Your only involvement is to give new customers the document wallet at handover. Use the personal action planner to ensure that you take full advantage of the programme.
Q. How long will customers stay on the programme?
A. Customers will continue to receive material throughout the ownership cycle. When they buy another product, they will begin a new cycle.

Encouraging training

If you operate sales training programmes, it is important to encourage full participation. This letter describes the benefits of training to individual sales people.

Winning sales people achieve their goals not just through personal sales skills, but through effective planning, sound product knowledge and a commitment to quality customer service. If you have the opportunity, desire and ability to achieve excellence in everything you do, results can be exceptional.

In practical terms, that means you will sell more, improve your personal performance and win higher levels of repeat business from satisfied customers. Continuous training and personal development are vital to ensure that you have the professional skills to win in a fiercely competitive marketplace.

If you want to get ahead in your sales career and make the most of the opportunities with the UK market leader for 18 consecutive years, talk to your sales manager about the courses that are most relevant to you. You'll be working with some of the best known training people in the industry on programmes that set the standard for the automotive business. You'll gain the confidence, the skills and the knowledge to deliver first-class service every time.

All we need is your commitment to training. After all, it's your future that's at stake.

Changes in company organisation

Internal changes can cause confusion in a sales force, so it is important to explain the full implications of a change. This letter announces the benefits of a reorganisation in a European software company.

I am very happy to welcome you to the new organisation. As you can see, we will share a common name and a new identity and these are the key to our success in the future. This brochure will tell you about the reasons for the change and your role in the future of the group.

By working together, we can draw on our individual strengths and achieve our goal of positioning the company as a leading European IT service supplier for the next decade. During the coming year, we will take a number of important steps towards achieving this goal.

First, we intend to establish a single, unified identity across Europe. This will help to distinguish us from other service providers and allow us to take advantage of the rapidly growing systems market. We will also prepare a family of new products and create a pan-European knowledge base so that we can benefit from shared experience.

To support our new identity, we are developing a new mission statement which clearly sets out our future direction. We are also working on market statements which reflect our reputation for leading edge technology combined with practical implementation. To strengthen our presence in the market, we will be applying the new identity to marketing support materials and trading materials. We will also be developing a range of advanced electronically-delivered marketing materials which will give us a great deal of flexibility within our distributed organisation.

All these initiatives are now under way and we are planning a public launch for our new identity in early September. In the meantime, we should be grateful if you would treat this information as company confidential. If you have any questions about the initiatives or if you would like to find out how they affect you, please talk to your country manager.

The new identity and the new marketing initiatives are the key to our success in the future. We hope you will give them your full support because it provides all of us with exciting new opportunities.

Self-assessment

1. Do you have a sales force communications policy?
2. Do you produce sales force guides to products and marketing programmes?
3. Do you encourage the sales force to participate in training?
4. Do you communicate changes in policy and organisation to the sales force?